PLIMOTH PLANTATION

PLIMOTH PLANTATION

DILLON PRESS
Parsippany, New Jersey

by Terry Janson Dunnahoo

To my grandson Ashton
with love

Photo Credits
Cover: Courtesy of Plimoth Plantation, Photo By Ted Curtin.

The Granger Collection: 24. © 1994 Northwind Pictures: 21. Courtesy of The Pilgrim Society, Plymouth, MA.: 18, 56. Courtesy of Plimoth Plantation, Photos by Ted Curtin: Title Page, 8, 11, 14, 23, 31, 34, 36, 40, 41, 47, 48, 50, 54, 58, 62, 67. Illustrations by Warren Budd & Associates, Ltd.: 6, 44.

Library of Congress Cataloging-in-Publication Data
Dunnahoo, Terry.
    Plimoth Plantation / by Terry Janson Dunnahoo.
      p. cm.—(Places in American History)
    Includes index.
    ISBN 0-87518-627-0
    1. Pilgrims (New Plymouth Colony)—Juvenile literature.
    2. Massachusetts—History—New Plymouth, 1620–1691—Juvenile litera-
ture. 3. Plimoth Plantation, Inc.—Guidebooks—Juvenile literature. [1.
Pilgrims (New Plymouth Colony) 2. Massachusetts—History—New
Plymouth, 1620–1691. 3. Plimoth Plantation, Inc.—Guides.] I. Title. II.
Series.
    F68.D93 1994
    974.4'8202—dc20   93-39625
Summary: A look at Plimoth Plantation, a living history museum popular with tourists who wish to learn about the Pilgrim settlement at Plymouth, Massachusetts.

Published by Dillon Press, an imprint of Silver Burdett Press.
A Simon & Schuster Company
299 Jefferson Road, Parsippany, NJ 07054

First Edition

Printed in the United States of America

10 9 8 7 6 5 4 3 2 1

CONTENTS

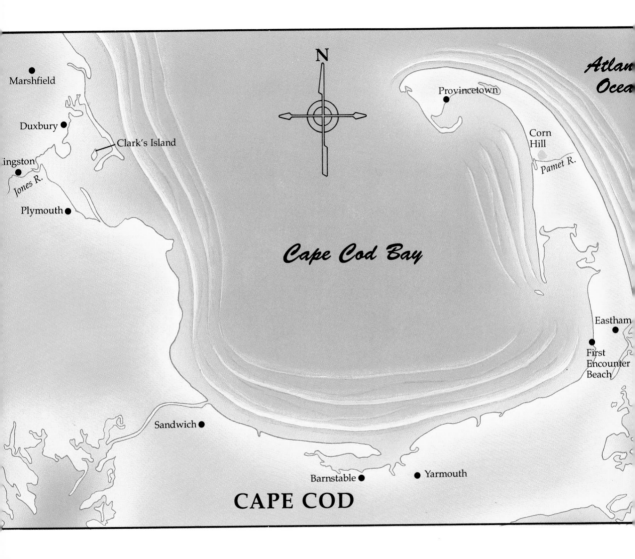

CHAPTER 1

A TROUBLED START

No one knows exactly when the Pilgrims celebrated the event we know as the first Thanksgiving, but the party was held sometime between September 21 and November 9 in 1621, and it lasted three days. It was a time to eat, play games, visit family and friends, and to say thanks, just as Thanksgiving is today.

The Pilgrims had sailed from England on the *Mayflower* the year before. Only two died from sickness along the way, but half died once they reached America. After the Native Americans taught the Pilgrims how to grow corn and where to hunt and fish in their new land, living conditions improved.

At the first Thanksgiving feast, the Pilgrim

A re-creation of the first Thanksgiving feast

governor, William Bradford, invited Sachem (Chief) Massasoit of the Wampanoag and his people to the party. About 90 men came to share the food. The Native Americans wore their traditional dress: feathers, furs, and animal skins.

The Pilgrims served wild turkeys, geese, and ducks that lived in the forests and migrated along the ocean shore, which four men had shot with muskets. The Native Americans brought to the feast five deer they had killed with arrows. The meat was boiled or roasted. Cod, shellfish, and eels were also available to boil or grill.

The Pilgrims ate carrots, turnips, onions, radishes, beets, and skirrets (another root vegetable) taken from the gardens they had planted the previous spring. They also cooked the native corn in breads and other ways.

The people who celebrated the first Thanksgiving did not have sweet corn on the cob or real popcorn, though. They ate hard flint corn as corn meal or as parched corn heated by the fire so it puffed up a little at the first Thanksgiving.

Cranberries grew wild and pumpkins were raised as a crop, but because sugar was rare no one made cranberry sauce or pumpkin pie for dessert. Instead the Pilgrims ate the wild fruits and nuts available at harvest time, such as beach plums, grapes, walnuts, hazelnuts, and perhaps blueberries dried by the Wampanoag. The Native Americans picked the berries in the late summer when they became ripe and dried them in the sun to eat in the fall and winter.

While servants, children, and the four surviving women cooked, Captain Myles Standish directed the men through their military drill in honor of the day. One man blew a trumpet and another beat a drum as the men marched. The soldiers fired their muskets and the Native men shot their arrows at targets. Everyone joined in.

On August 5, 1620, the Pilgrims had left Southampton, England, to sail to the New World on the ships *Speedwell* and *Mayflower*. Soon the *Speedwell* began to leak. The Pilgrims put into

A painting of the Mayflower, *the ship that brought the Pilgrims to the New World*

Exeter, England, to fix the ship, and then they sailed away again. But the *Speedwell* sprang more leaks, so the Pilgrims had to go back a second time. Some people then decided not to go to the New World.

Finally, on September 6, 1620, the *Mayflower* set sail from Plymouth, England, this time without the *Speedwell*. One hundred two passengers and about 30 sailors were aboard, including Master (Captain) Christopher Jones, Giles Heale the surgeon, and the cook. Some male passengers sailed without their families.

About half of the passengers journeyed to the New World because they were not allowed to practice their religion freely. They were called Separatists. Others went because they could not find work or land in England. Some left home for adventure. In England, land was largely owned by a few rich people, and most people could not buy nor even rent it. The Pilgrims were willing to make the dangerous trip across the Atlantic to worship freely and become landowners.

On this crowded ship, people could take only a few belongings. Everything else was sold before they left to pay for their voyage. Families brought few toys, though most brought their precious Bibles.

During the first month at sea, the wind filled the sails, but the sea was calm and the sky clear. But then the weather turned bad, and the sea became rough and dangerous. Almost everyone on board became seasick.

The ocean waves tossed the *Mayflower* around as if it were a toy. The ship's timbers cracked and creaked. Water washed across the decks and leaked below, soaking passengers, their clothes, and their belongings. The waves sometimes rose higher than houses. One passenger, John Howland, was swept overboard, but he was able to grab a topsail rope and was pulled back on board.

Some people told Master Jones that they wanted to go back to England. He calmed their fears by telling them that the *Mayflower* was a

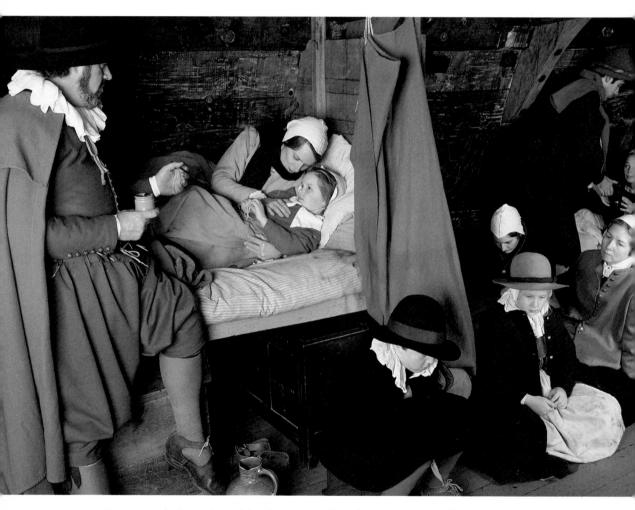

Passengers aboard the Mayflower *endured cramped, unpleasant living conditions.*

strong, safe ship. Besides, he said, they were already more than halfway through their trip.

Living conditions on the ship were terrible for the passengers. There was no heat, it was always wet and dark below deck, and there was nothing to do. The passengers were dirty, since they could not wash themselves or their smelly clothes. The sea water was no good for washing or drinking. They wore the same clothes day after day and slept in them at night as the days grew colder. Some people slept in hammocks or on waterproof leather mattresses. Others slept on piles of damp straw on the decks.

After a while the drinking water became smelly and unpleasant. Most people, however, drank beer as they did at home, including the children. The Pilgrims' diet was not very interesting or healthy. Because they did not have refrigeration to keep food from spoiling, everything was dried or salted. Passengers ate salted beef or pork, dried peas and oatmeal, salt fish, and hard ship's biscuit made without shortening or salt. Once the storms began, the food was served cold because the ship moved like a rocking horse and building cooking fires was too dangerous.

Without enough sleep, fresh drinking water, and healthy food, the passengers and crew became sick. The Pilgrims were sad when the doctor's servant died of fever. They were happy, though, when a boy named Oceanus was born to Elizabeth and Stephen Hopkins.

Finally, on the morning of November 9, 1620, the Pilgrims sighted land. There were no friends present to greet them on the shore. There were no houses to live in or stores to shop in. But the woods grew right down to the shoreline, the sky was filled with birds, and the sea abounded with fish.

The Pilgrims wanted to get off the *Mayflower* after their long and difficult voyage. They were eager to find foods and brooks filled with fresh water. They wanted to wash their clothes and themselves. They longed to run on the dry beach. But all this had to wait.

The ship was not where it was supposed to be. The *Mayflower* had been hired to take the colonists to the "northern parts of Virginia around the mouth of the Hudson River." But the ship was too far east. It had landed on Cape Cod in what is now Massachusetts. It was very late in the year to go much farther. As the Pilgrims stared at the shore, they wondered what to do next.

This painting shows a meeting of Chief Massasoit with the Pilgrims.

CHAPTER 2

HUNGRY DAYS AND COLD NIGHTS

The Pilgrims were not the first people to see the land that is now Massachusetts. Native Americans had been living on this land for many years before they saw ships coming from Europe. Sometimes European sailors came ashore to barter, or trade, with the native peoples. Often, these bartering visitors had diseases new to the native people. The Native Americans caught diseases, became sick, and died in great numbers. There had once been over 20,000 Wampanoag. But by the time the Pilgrims saw Cape Cod, there were only a few thousand alive.

The explorer John Cabot had claimed the land for England in 1498, even though the Native Americans were already living there. As more and more ships came, Native Americans grew to distrust these men who sometimes attacked and carried them away in the ships. In 1602, Bartholomew Gosnold saw land that looked like an arm reaching into the sea and named it Cape Cod. Later, John Smith explored the land he called New England. In 1616 he published a detailed description, including maps, of what he had seen.

Unlike some other explorers, Captain Smith did not take any Native Americans back to England with him. Captain Thomas Hunt, however, took 27 Wampanoag away in chains and sold them in Spain as slaves. One of the Wampanoag, named Tisquantum, escaped from Spain and went to England, where he learned to speak English.

In 1618, Captain Thomas Dermer brought Tisquantum, who was also known as Squanto, to Newfoundland in America. When they returned to Squanto's native land in New England, they found that all of his people were dead of

THE PORTRAICTUER OF CAPTAYNE IOHN SMITH / ADMIRALL OF NEW ENGLAND

A portrait of Captain John Smith

European diseases. Captain Dermer went on to Virginia in 1620, but Squanto decided to stay with Massasoit, sachem of the Wampanoag people.

Although the Pilgrims had learned about Native Americans from John Smith and other explorers' books, the travelers could not help but wonder about the natives. Would these people be friends or enemies?

When the *Mayflower* reached land on November 9, 1620, the Pilgrims found they had a different problem. Should they go ashore at Cape Cod, or should they go on to the mouth of the Hudson River? The Pilgrim leaders decided to continue their voyage to the Hudson, where the colonists' charter gave them permission to settle.

On its way once again, the *Mayflower* found the water full of dangerous reefs and rocks that threatened to sink the ship. Master Jones fought to keep the *Mayflower* off the rocks. He steered the ship to safety back towards Cape Cod.

The *Mayflower* anchored in Cape Cod

(Provincetown) Harbor on November 11. That same day 41 men signed the Mayflower Compact. As their charter was no good in New England, the Compact contained rules under which they could govern themselves until they got a new charter. It remained the law in Plymouth Colony until 1629, when they finally got ownership of their land at Plymouth. John Carver was elected governor.

On the afternoon of November 11, some men rowed ashore in the ship's longboat, which was the small boat that brought people to and from the larger ship. The water was too shallow to bring even the longboat close to the shore. Dressed in armor, they had to wade through the icy water.

The explorers were disappointed to find no running brooks of fresh water and that the ponds were somewhat salty. This water was not good for cooking or drinking or farming. The explorers were, however, able to cut trees for firewood. While working, they watched for Native

In this painting, William Bradford prepares to sign the Mayflower Compact.

Americans but did not see any. Then the men carried the wood through the icy water to the longboat and back to the *Mayflower*.

It was now time for the colonists to come ashore, bringing pieces of a larger boat, or shallop, to put together. The men cut more firewood and looked for fresh water. The women used the pond water to wash clothes and hung them to dry over bushes. Children played and found mussels in the shallow water. At the end of the day everyone went back to sleep on the ship.

Because the explorers had not yet found fresh water, William Bradford, Myles Standish, and other men went looking for water again. Dressed in heavy armor and carrying muskets and swords, they marched through the woods, ready for any encounters. As they set up camp, the explorers saw their first Native Americans, who turned and ran. The men tried to catch up with them, but the natives escaped.

The next day the men finally found some springs of fresh water and drank it "with as

much delight as ever we drank in all our lives."
The explorers then discovered a large cornfield
and a burial ground. They also found buried in
the ground "a fine great basket full of every fair
corn of this year—some yellow and some red and
other ears mixed with blue." They called this
place Corn Hill.

The following morning, hungry, wet, and
tired, the explorers went back to the ship and
showed the others the corn they had found,
which could be planted in their fields. The
Pilgrims agreed that the corn should sustain
them in their new homeland. But not everyone
could agree where the new settlement should be
built.

While the explorers had been searching the
land, the carpenters had been on the beach working to repair the *Mayflower*'s shallop. Shallops
are boats about 30 feet long that can be rowed or
sailed. The shallop on the *Mayflower* had been
damaged by people climbing over the sections
during the crossing. When the shallop was fixed,

Master Jones and more than 30 men climbed aboard and set out to find a place to build the colonists' new homes. They shivered in their wet clothes and pulled icicles from their whiskers.

While some men followed the coast in the shallop, the rest searched inland for miles. Snow fell all day and freezing winds blew. The men's armor was heavy, and the clothes worn underneath became wet and icy on their bodies. The explorers found shelter under pine trees and built campfires, but they still shivered through the night. If they did not build permanent homes soon, no one would survive the harsh New England winter.

The next day some men went back to the ship, while the others stayed ashore. They shot some geese and ducks for supper after they marched through the snow all day. They found some Native American houses but did not see anyone. Some of the explorers wanted to settle in this area, since the land was good for farming. Others thought the harbor was not deep enough and there was not enough fresh water. The men argued. Finally they decided to return to the *Mayflower* to discuss with the others what they had seen.

Aboard the ship the explorers were told that one of the Billington boys had shot a loaded musket in his father's cabin and had played with homemade fireworks near open barrels of gunpowder. If any sparks had hit the barrels, there would have been a serious explosion and fire.

Although some people wanted to go north to a distant place to settle, the Pilgrims agreed they had traveled enough. The ship was crowded. Many people were sick with coughs and fever. They were all cold and were afraid their food would run low. It was decided that they would settle somewhere near Cape Cod Bay.

CHAPTER 3

A HOME AT LAST

Robert Coppin, the Mayflower's pilot, told the Pilgrims about a good harbor he had visited earlier, which Captain John Smith had called "Plymouth" on his map. John Carver, Myles Standish, William Bradford, and some others sailed in the shallop to investigate. The water was icy and rough but the shallop struggled through.

When they landed, they saw some native men cutting up a small whale, but the men ran away. After looking around, the explorers set up camp. They saw the smoke of some fires in the distance, but they were too tired to go and check them out. Some men stayed awake to guard the camp while the others slept. In the morning the men explored farther inland and found good farming land and streams of fresh water. They did not see any sign of the Native Americans until later on, when they found a number of native houses and fields but no people.

As the explorers made camp that night on the shore near the shallop, they were glad that they had not met any hostile native men. Again, they were too tired to do anything but sleep. During the night, cries awoke them. Some men said the cries came from Native Americans. Others thought the cries were from wolves or foxes. The explorers shot their muskets and the cries stopped.

In the morning the explorers heard the cries again. This time, showers of arrows whizzed past them. In the early-morning darkness, the explorers could not see who was behind the trees. The cries grew louder and some arrows hit coats that were hung up. The Pilgrims shot their muskets at the shadowy figures amid the trees. The bowmen howled and ran away. The soldiers followed, but the Native Americans had vanished.

At First Encounter Beach the Pilgrims shot their muskets at the Native American bowmen whose arrows had whizzed by them.

The explorers called this place First Encounter Beach and went back to the shallop carrying bundles of arrows. That afternoon they found the harbor John Smith had named Plymouth and spent their first Sunday there on an island in the rain and snow.

When the men did go ashore at Plymouth on Monday, December 11, wrote William Bradford, they were happy with what they saw. In his journal Bradford called Plymouth a hopeful place. There were several brooks of fresh water, fertile land, and a harbor to shelter the *Mayflower*. The explorers hurried back to the ship to bring the good news.

They did not get a chance to celebrate, however. Bradford's wife, Dorothy, had fallen overboard and drowned. More people were sick and several died. When the *Mayflower* followed the shallop's course into Plymouth Harbor, many Pilgrims were too sick to go ashore.

The bad diet and their exposure to the cold, wet weather had worn them down. The colonists buried their dead, but they could not take time to mourn. They had to build houses or they would all die before spring.

The men started building the Common House at Plymouth on Christmas Day in 1620. They cut down trees, chopped them into timbers, or sawed and split them into boards. Then, working in snow and sleet, they raised the house frames, thatched the roofs with reeds, and put clay walls between the framing timbers. Until they got their first house done, they had to return to the *Mayflower* each night.

By January 14, when a fire burned off the roof of their Common House, there were enough shelters built for most of the workers to stay on shore each night. The fire that they had lit on the dirt floor of the Common House had sent a spark into the thatch roof. Luckily no one was hurt in the fire.

The colonists decided to build houses for 19 families, so fewer houses had to be built. Each family would take in several other colonists. But

Using timbers and boards from trees they had cut down, the colonists raised house frames.

even meeting this goal was difficult, because the cold and wet made all but six or seven people so sick that they could not work much, if at all. More settlers died each week.

Every day except Sundays the colonists worked on their houses. They found that the rain washed away their clay walls, which had to be covered with clapboards. The wind blew in through chinks in the walls and through the glassless windows. Rain got down the wooden chimneys into the fireplaces, which were the only source of heat. The fireplace of the building where many of the sick people were, set the reed roof of that building on fire, but no great harm was done.

There was still enough food, but it was the same dry food they had on the *Mayflower*, and they had problems obtaining fresh supplies. The colonists were not used to shooting animals with their muskets, and their fish hooks were the wrong size. Everyone was weak from the poor diet. So many had died that the settlers decided

The roofs of the colonists' houses were thatched with reeds.

that the dead should be buried secretly at night. They were afraid that the Native Americans would attack if they knew how few colonists were left to defend the settlement.

Master Jones brought cannons from the *Mayflower* which were put on the Fort Hill (later called Burial Hill) above the village. Some were pointed toward the sea to protect the settlement against enemy ships. Other cannons were pointed towards the woods to protect the settlement against the Native Americans.

Then in March 1621, a Native American came boldly out of the woods and walked right into the settlement. Some colonists ran away. Others moved towards him.

"Welcome, Englishmen," the Native American said. He told them that his name was Samoset. The colonists were surprised to hear a Native American speaking English. Samoset said that he had learned English from the fishermen and traders who came to his home in Maine. Samoset and the colonists talked a long time. The settlers told him about some tools that had been stolen when they were left in the woods at lunch time one day.

Samoset said that some of Sachem Massasoit's people had taken the tools. When the colonists explained to Samoset that they needed their tools back, he agreed to get them from the men who had taken them. Samoset stayed with the settlers that night and left in the morning. When he visited again with some other Native American men, they brought back the tools.

Later Samoset returned with Tisquantum, or Squanto, to meet the colonists. Then Sachem Massasoit came with his people to meet Governor Carver. Governor Carver and Massasoit made a peace treaty and agreed not to attack but to help each other.

Squanto came to live with the settlers in his old home, which had been called Patuxet before the English renamed it Plymouth. He acted as their translator when dealing with Massasoit and his people. He taught them where to fish and how to hunt deer and turkeys. He showed them which native plants were good to eat and which were good for making medicine. Most importantly, he taught the settlers how to properly plant the corn they had taken from Corn Hill.

Squanto showed the colonists where they could catch great numbers of herring. And he taught them how to use the herring to fertilize the small mounds where the kernels of corn were planted in native fashion. Without Squanto's help, the Pilgrims might never have had the good harvest that made the first Thanksgiving possible.

The children of Plymouth Colony did not have much time to play. They had to work alongside their parents as best they could. The tended the food cooking in the fireplace, and they weeded the kitchen gardens. They sewed napkins and mended shirts. The also picked up sticks as kindling for the fires and helped scare off the birds from the cornfields.

Even with the help of the Native Americans, half the Pilgrims died. Yet when the *Mayflower*

Squanto taught the colonists how to use herring to fertilize the mounds where the kernels of corn were planted.

The children of Plymouth Colony worked alongside their parents at home and in the fields.

sailed back to England on April 5, 1621, none of the survivors wanted to go with the ship. A few weeks later, Governor Carver died of sunstroke, and his wife died soon after. They were the last people to die that year. William Bradford became the second governor of Plymouth Colony.

Only four wives lived through the first winter: Elinore Billington, Mary Brewster, Elizabeth Hopkins, and Susanna White. The children whose parents had died moved in with other families. Peregrine White, who had been born at Cape Cod aboard the *Mayflower,* went to live with his mother and new stepfather, Edward Winslow. By fall only 7 houses of the 19 originally planned were built since so many families had died.

Despite all these hardships, the settlers planted their gardens as well as 26 acres of field crops during the first spring and watched them grow through the summer. Then in the fall, they invited Massasoit and his people to their harvest party. It was a time of thanksgiving, a time to thank God and their Native American friends for the help they had given, and to celebrate having survived the first year in the New World.

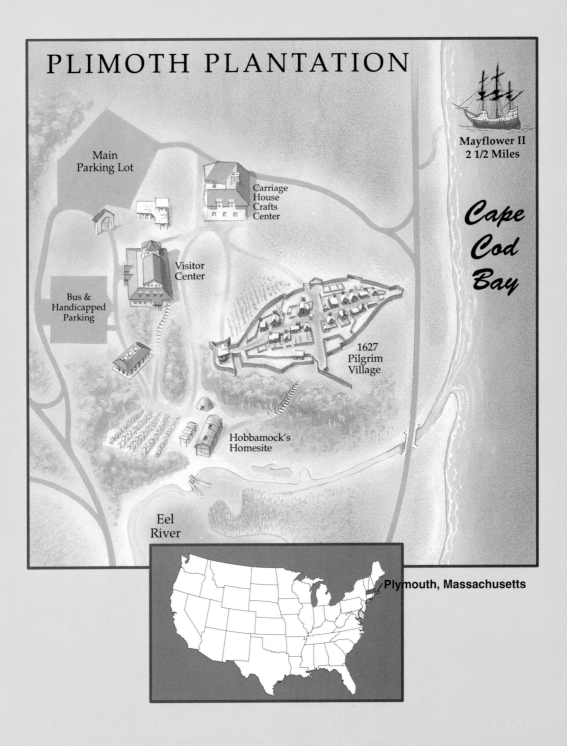

PLIMOTH PLANTATION

Main
Parking Lot

Carriage
House
Crafts
Center

Visitor
Center

Bus &
Handicapped
Parking

1627
Pilgrim
Village

Hobbamock's
Homesite

Eel
River

Mayflower II
2 1/2 Miles

Cape
Cod
Bay

Plymouth, Massachusetts

CHAPTER 4

A DREAM COMES TRUE

In crossing the Atlantic Ocean, the Pilgrims showed great courage and perseverance. Many people have written stories and poems about them and their historic voyage. Many years later a boy named Henry Hornblower II was inspired by these stories. He spent almost every summer in Plymouth with his family. Henry, known as Harry, walked through the streets and wondered how the Pilgrims had lived in Plymouth.

As a boy, he worked in Plymouth with archaeologists. They found dishes, tools, and other artifacts. When Harry was older, he went to work in his family's investment business in Boston. But he had a dream of building a living museum to show how the colonists had lived. In December

Henry Hornblower II

1945, Harry talked his father into giving $20,000 to the Pilgrim Society to make the dream of a living museum come true. That $20,000 was the beginning of Plimoth Plantation. This spelling was the one William Bradford used when he wrote in his journal.

By 1948, a reproduction of the colony's First House, also called the Common House, was started near Plymouth Rock. During the first year 390,000 people visited the house. Harry and others wanted to give visitors more to see and learn about at Plimoth Plantation. To do this, they needed more land. They decided on some land along the Eel River. In 1953, the Fort/ Meetinghouse was built on the Plymouth Waterfront. In 1955, the 1627 House was built near the First House. The 1627 House showed visitors a house style the Pilgrims had used once they had become settled.

To recreate Plimoth Plantation, historians studied Governor Bradford's journal, other Pilgrims' accounts, and the writings of other visi-

Archaeologists carefully excavated areas in and around Plymouth.

tors to Plymouth. For 40 years, archaeologists dug in and around Plymouth. They found more than 350,000 objects, including pottery, coins, and farm tools. They studied these artifacts and read books about how the colonists lived. Then they made reproductions of the houses, furniture, and clothing of the Pilgrims.

People who work at Plimoth Plantation today do everyday jobs in the same way the colonists did them. They wear the same kinds of clothes the Pilgrims wore, which were all handmade. They cook food in large open fireplaces and make barrels and baskets. They put reed thatch on roofs and chop wood for fireplaces. While doing all these tasks, the museum workers use the same kinds of tools used by the Pilgrims in the seventeenth century.

At Plimoth Plantation you can meet people dressed as William Bradford and John Billington. You can also meet Myles Standish and John and Priscilla Alden, three colonists celebrated in Henry Wadsworth Longfellow's famous poem

Workers at Plimoth Plantation bake and do other everyday jobs in the same way that the colonists did.

"The Courtship of Miles Standish." All of these Pilgrim characters will tell you how they felt when they left England and explain how scared they were during the trip across the Atlantic. They will also relate how sad they were when a friend or family member died.

The houses in Plimoth Plantation are built just as the colonists built their homes. Dirt paths lead up to the plain-looking houses. Uneven fences surround the buildings to keep cows, sheep, and goats from going inside.

In the spring, you can watch workers at Plimoth Plantation plant gardens. In the summer, the people weed and water. And in the fall, they bring in their crops. Everyday chores are important, too, such as milking cows and goats, shearing sheep, and making bread.

There are a total of 15 homes at Plimoth Plantation, including a reproduction of John Howland's house. He was the servant of John Carver, the colony's first governor. After everyone in the Carver family died in the spring of 1621,

Peter Browne House

John Howland married Elizabeth Tilley, also a *Mayflower* passenger. Across the street is Peter Browne's house. He was one of the unmarried men who sailed to the new land for adventure.

Outside the village walls you can watch two-man teams saw logs into boards. There is also a large building in which to store hay. Its roof can be moved up or down to either protect the hay or to let it dry. There is even a building for cattle, which in England was called a beasthouse.

Not far from Myles Standish's house is the Fort/Meetinghouse. The original building was started in 1622. It served as the courthouse, jail, and church for the Pilgrims. Every Sunday until his death in 1643, William Brewster gave a sermon there. The fort was built to protect the colony against enemies. There were six cannons on the roof. Guards kept watch at night.

Near the village is Hobbamock's Homesite. Hobbamock was a Native American who lived with his family near Plimoth Plantation while helping the colonists. At the homesite there is the

Hobbamock's Homesite with its Arbor, an area for outdoor work

Arbor, a sheltered place for outdoor work made from saplings and boughs. You can also visit three houses there: the main house, called the Neesquttow; a smaller one for women, sometimes called the Wetuomemess; and another for other people, known as the Puttuckakaun. You can see corn, squash, and tobacco in the garden. These are the crops the Native Americans planted in the 1600s.

Burial Hill is where William Bradford and his family are buried. The poet Henry Wadsworth Longfellow, a relative of John Alden's, often came to the cemetery.

Not far from Burial Hill is Cole's Hill, where the colonists buried their dead in unmarked graves. A memorial to the *Mayflower* passengers and a statue of Chief Massasoit are found there.

At the bottom of Cole's Hill is Plymouth Rock. For years, people have told stories about how the Pilgrims stepped off the *Mayflower* onto Plymouth Rock as a way of getting to dry land. Although some of the Pilgrims may have stepped

Burial Hill, where William Bradford and his family are buried

on the rock, their feet would have been wet long before they touched it. Every time that people from the *Mayflower* came ashore to work on the Common House or to hunt animals for food, they had to wade through water part of the way.

For years, visitors could step on the rock and pretend they had just come from England on the *Mayflower*. Over the years, however, souvenir hunters have chipped 3,000 pounds off the rock. Now, to protect what is left, the rock is under a columned monument and is surrounded by a fence to protect it from weather and tourists. Engraved in the rock is the date 1620 to remind everyone of the year the Pilgrims came ashore.

Mayflower II

CHAPTER 5

THE *MAYFLOWER* SAILS AGAIN

Not far from the houses at Plimoth Plantation is *Mayflower II*, a reproduction of the original *Mayflower*. This ship is another part of Plimoth Plantation's living museum. Aboard the ship, guides take the roles of the original passengers and crew. Some wear the kinds of clothing that sailors wore, while others dress as Pilgrims.

The person who had thought of the idea to build a replica of the *Mayflower* was an Englishman, Warwick Charlton. He thought the ship would be a way to thank the United States for helping Great Britain fight during World War II.

Several people in Great Britain got together to talk about building the ship. In March 1955 an Englishman named John Lowe came to the

United States to talk about the project. He asked the directors of Plimoth Plantation if a replica of the *Mayflower* could be part of the living museum.

Lowe was surprised to learn that several years earlier, in 1951, the directors had decided to build a replica of the famous ship themselves. William A. Baker, a naval architect, had already designed a model of part of the hull, so it was agreed that the British builders should use his design. The plan called for *Mayflower II* to be built in England and then sailed across the Atlantic to Plimoth Plantation.

Many people thought *Mayflower II* was a poor idea. Some said it would cost too much money. Others wondered who would sail it. Sailors in the 1950s did not know how to sail this kind of ship. Some newspaper writers said *Mayflower II* had only a 50 percent chance of making it across the Atlantic.

But many people thought those odds were not so bad. The British raised the money to pay for the ship, and they studied blueprints used to build seventeenth-century ships to verify the accuracy of Baker's design. Alan Villiers of Australia was chosen as captain of *Mayflower II*. He was an expert sailor who had written about ships and sailing.

Villiers immediately started making plans to get *Mayflower II*, its crew, and passengers safely across the Atlantic. Thousands of people asked to sail on the ship. Two lucky young men were selected to work as ship's boys on *Mayflower II*. The Boys Club of America chose Joseph Meany, Jr., of Massachusetts, and a similar club across the Atlantic chose Graham Nunn, of England.

One person who wanted to be part of the crew but was turned down tried to stow away on the boat. While *Mayflower II* was still in the harbor, the man was found hiding behind some chests stored on one of the decks. He was put on a boat filled with photographers who had followed the ship. When the boat went back to shore, the stowaway returned with them.

Ship's boys Joseph Meany, Jr., of Massachusetts (left) and Graham Nunn of England (right) with Captain Alan Villiers

Mayflower II left Plymouth, England, on April 20, 1957. For two days there was not much wind to move the ship. The sailors were disappointed. But while they waited for stronger winds, the sailors learned how to better run the ship. They even practiced putting the sails up and down in darkness. This was an important task to learn because the ship had little electricity.

The only light available near the old-fashioned compass was a candle lantern. Captain Villiers wondered how Master Christopher Jones had found America with that kind of compass. But Captain Villiers himself was not worried about finding America: He had modern instruments to guide *Mayflower II*. This ship also had life rafts and two-way radios—things the original ship did not have. With these modern inventions, *Mayflower II* passengers would never know the danger that the Pilgrims in 1620 experienced.

Captain Villiers planned to take the northern route to Massachusetts. But 11 days out of England, gale winds moved the ship south. As a result, *Mayflower II* used the same route that Christopher Columbus had used in 1492.

The crew liked the warm weather and the calm waters of the southern route, but then, near Bermuda, a storm hit. Many people got seasick on the rocking ship. The ship had medicine to control seasickness, but it was not supposed to be used. Some of the passengers were so sick that they used the medicine anyway. When the Pilgrims became seasick on their trip, however, they had to suffer without medicine.

The rocking ship made it hard for people to walk. Even the ship's cat, Felix, had trouble walking around, and the rocking at first kept him awake. But he quickly learned to sleep while the ship rocked and rolled. Felix ate canned fish and got plenty of milk to drink. The ship's third mate even made a life jacket for Felix. No one cared as well for the cat on the original *Mayflower*, who had to drink up spilled beer and hunt for mice to eat. And Felix drank lime juice when *Mayflower II* cook served it to the sailors and passengers so that they wouldn't get scurvy. Scurvy is a disease that makes a person's gums bleed and teeth fall out. It was a common illness of sailors in the 1700s, who did not have enough fresh fruit and vegetables to eat during voyages.

The ship's cook baked bread three times a week on an oil stove instead of in a brick oven like the one the Pilgrims used. But some water was provided on *Mayflower II* the same way as on the original ship: When rain fell, containers on deck collected the water.

The *Mayflower II* reached Provincetown, at the tip of Cape Cod, on June 12, 1957, and arrived at Plymouth the next day. It had taken 66 days for the original Pilgrims to reach the New World. It took *Mayflower II* only 53 days to reach America. Nobody had greeted the first *Mayflower*, but blimps, Coast Guard cutters, and dozens of smaller ships escorted *Mayflower II* into the harbor. More than 1,000 people met the historic ship, including Chief Wildhorse, a Wampanoag Native American.

When the Pilgrims stepped off their ship, they were hungry and had no fresh food left. When the sailors and passengers came off *Mayflower II*, there were parties and more food than they could eat.

Today, visitors can talk to people on *Mayflower II*. Museum guides play the parts of sailors and passengers who sailed on the first ship. They will tell you how terrible the crossing was from England. Some will say they want to go back to England. Others cannot wait to begin building homes at Plimoth Plantation.

On *Mayflower II* you can see the Round House, where Master Christopher Jones and his men lived while they sailed the *Mayflower*. The steerage was where important passengers slept. The space was small, but it was less crowded than the 'tween decks. Most of the 102 passengers were crowded into the 'tween decks during the crossing of 1620.

Alongside *Mayflower II* there is a 33-foot shallop that looks like the shallop brought by the Pilgrims on the first *Mayflower*. William Baker drew the plans for the shallop. It was built in Plymouth, Massachusetts, so that *Mayflower II* would not have to carry it to the United States.

Guides aboard Mayflower II, *dressed as the ship's passengers and crew, tell tourists about the crossing.*

When you finish your visit to *Mayflower II* and you walk off the ship, imagine there is nothing around you but sand and trees. Only you and the other Pilgrims are there. Many people are sick. You have no idea what the coming days will bring. Imagine all of this and then you will know how brave and strong and determined the Pilgrims were to sail to the New World.

Visitor Information

Hours
April through November, all exhibits: 9:00 A.M. to 5:00 P.M.
Pilgrim Village site: 9:00 A.M. to 5:00 P.M.; Mayflower II: 9:00 A.M. to 7:00 P.M. in July and August.

Admission
General Admission ticket including *Mayflower II*: $18.50 for adults, $11.00 for children ages 5 through 12, free for children under 5.
Pilgrim Village site: $15.00 for adults, $9.00 for children 5 through 12, free for children under 5.
Mayflower II: $5.75 for adults, $3.75 for children.

Visitor Center
The Visitor Center prepares visitors for their time travel to the 1620s. There are exhibition galleries and a crafts center in the Carriage House. An audiovisual presentation gives an overview of what to see at Plimoth Plantation. The Peabody Picnic Pavilion is a fun place to eat and relax.

Tours
Visitors walk through the 1627 Plimoth Village and can then stroll through the Eel River Nature Walk to Hobbamock's Homesite to learn about Native American culture in the seventeenth century and today.

Visitors with general admission tickets can board *Mayflower II*. Aboard, costumed guides talk about what it was like to sail on the *Mayflower* and tell how hard it was to build homes and grow food in the new land.

Special Events
Seasonal activities include planting, house building, harvesting, food preparation, and militia drills, all done by costumed workers.

Additional Information
Plimoth Plantation
P.O. Box 1620
Plymouth, MA 02362-1620
Phone (508) 746-1622

Index